HELLER

SELECTED STUDIES

Opus 45 and Opus 46

Edited and Recorded by William Westney

To access companion recorded performances online, visit:
www.halleonard.com/mylibrary

Enter Code
1431-1342-1335-5548

On the cover:
Der Morgen
by Valentin Ruths
(1875)

ISBN 978-0-634-09839-0

G. SCHIRMER, *Inc.*

DISTRIBUTED BY

HAL•LEONARD®
CORPORATION

7777 W. BLUEMOUND RD. P.O. BOX 13819 MILWAUKEE, WI 53213

www.musicsalesclassical.com
www.halleonard.com

The price of this publication includes access to companion recorded performances online, for download or streaming, using the unique code found on the title page. Visit **www.halleonard.com/mylibrary** and enter the access code.

CONTENTS

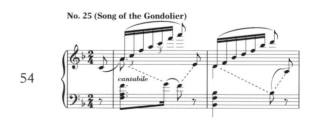

HISTORICAL NOTES

STEPHEN HELLER (1813-1888)

Stephen Heller was born in Budapest on May 15, 1813. From a very early age he had begged his parents to let him take piano lessons. One day, as he later described in a letter to Robert Schumann, his father brought home half-a-dozen players from the local regimental band and said: "Here, Stephen, I've brought you some people who understand this stuff; take your pick. The one you like best shall be your piano teacher."

One of these, a clarinetist, Bohemian by birth, proved satisfactory. Several weeks later the boy secretly wrote, in honor of his teacher, a set of variations on a Bohemian song. Here is his own description, written several years later, of its first performance:

> I had written almost everything *tutti*—violin, 'cello, flute, bassoon, and drums (I was seven years old). I'll never forget it! Imagine over a dozen players in a little room, with an audience consisting of the proud conductor of the regimental band in the seat of honor on the sofa, and a few of my teachers from school—and then the jumble of my composition! All my classmates... had been invited, since we did not have any music stand and they had to hold up the music for the players. Father ran around in seventh heaven.

After this triumph he was given lessons by the choirmaster in one of the big Budapest churches. Soon he made a public appearance at one of the local theaters, playing, with his teacher, a two-piano concerto by Dussek.

His father, perhaps too eager to make money out of his son's talents, sent him to Vienna, where he studied briefly under Carl Czerny, and then for a longer time under Anton Halm. Through Halm he met Beethoven and Schubert. Soon, at the age of 13, Heller was giving concerts in Vienna. And at the age of 15 he was going on long concert tours through central Europe. On these tours he met many of the great musicians of the world. One winter in Warsaw, for example, he became acquainted with Chopin, and gave a concert jointly with Paganini.

But after five years of this life of a traveling concert artist—a period which he later spoke of as "five murderous years, a nomad life, restless, hopeless, aimless"— he found that he could not go on; though he was then only 17, he felt completely worn out. As he was at Augsburg when his concert tour thus reached a standstill, he remained at Augsburg for eight years, as teacher and as musician for Count Fugger, a nobleman whose family had long been active in the cultural life of that city. While there he began a correspondence with Robert Schumann, which ripened into a fine and lasting friendship between the two composers.

From Augsburg he went— at the advice of Friedrich Kalkbrenner—to Paris. Heller's first years in Paris were very hard. Kalkbrenner was to have been his teacher and mentor, but Heller—like Chopin—soon found that Kalkbrenner had nothing to teach him. For several years he supported himself by whatever arranging, teaching, and performing he could find to do. Being of a naturally retiring nature, he had a difficult struggle at first. But after about five or six years he became established; and the fact that he continued to live in Paris for almost fifty years (*i.e.*, until his death, on January 15, 1888) indicates the contentment and security that he found for himself there. During those Paris years he was in intimate contact with many of the leading musicians of Europe—Chopin, Berlioz, Halévy, Alkan, Panofka, David, Wolff, Seligman, and a whole group of musicians centering around Karl Hallé.

In the course of his long and fruitful life, Heller wrote several hundred piano pieces, classified under some 150 opus numbers. Of these, the *Studies*, Opus 45 & Opus 46 have particular vitality. Written in 1844, six years after Heller had gone to Paris, they thus mark the time of Heller making a secure place for himself in that great city of music. He was still a young man, yet one who had already behind him extensive experience as a concert artist, teacher, and composer.

—Willis Wager
reprinted from the 1942 G. Schirmer edition

PERFORMANCE NOTES

Overview of the Works

Etudes for piano can accomplish many different things, just as piano lessons themselves can have various goals. The most successful etudes build technical mastery in specific ways, while providing rich musical delights for player and listener alike.

The well-crafted, captivating works of Stephen Heller meet this high standard virtually every time. Loved and admired by contemporary teachers and students who know them, these studies were spoken of glowingly in their own time by the likes of Schumann, Chopin, and Mendelssohn. The consensus through the ages seems to be that Heller was an extraordinarily gifted artist of great refinement. His etudes are treasures, creative and graceful in style, and they certainly deserve to be widely played and enjoyed.

One reason that students respond to the pieces immediately is quite simple: they feel good under the hands. Clearly, Heller possessed a thorough understanding of how piano playing works. The studies, as a group, are full of textural variety and thus make colorful recital pieces, especially when their descriptive titles are used. As we delve further into each piece, subtle compositional touches reveal themselves; for many students this adds another satisfaction—that of playing stylish, mature music. It might be said that Heller complicated things just a bit on occasion by adding extra details and variations; but this is always done in the interest of formal elegance. Etudes, after all, are effective when they build a whole piece on one technical component, but this can often lead to monotony. Heller knew just how to keep such compositions intriguing until the last bar.

Because they can initiate the developing pianist so naturally into a certain sophistication of playing, Heller's etudes provide excellent stepping-stones to the great romantic works of Chopin, Mendelssohn, and others. They develop color, fluency, power, and poetic musicality. Many have that always-delightful quality of sounding rather brilliant without actually being too difficult.

It isn't always easy to find satisfying works by the great composers that are technically approachable for the intermediate, advancing pianist. Many of Mendelssohn's *Songs Without Words*, for example, are much more technically problematic than they sound, calling for a large hand-span and expertise in handling complex textural writing. Studying them can thus be quite frustrating for the developing pianist. Heller's studies, which greatly resemble the Mendelssohn pieces in style, are not only more playable, but so attractive in every way that if one were to pretend that they actually *were* pieces from *Songs Without Words*, one would easily imagine them to be among the most popular and beloved of the set.

Notes on the Present Edition

A decision had to be made about the descriptive titles. Heller did not assign them to the pieces, but, as often happens, programmatic names appeared in certain historical editions and simply "stuck." The names are used inconsistently as well; the same piece that is called "The Avalanche" appears as "Goblin's Frolic" in another edition. By and large, though, the most commonly used titles are appropriate and evocative, even inspired at times ("Celestial Voices," "Il Penseroso," "Shimmering Waters"). In many cases, these images lend a particular shape to the music, which actually helps one's technique to feel purposeful and secure. Therefore we have included them for your consideration.

All the studies in this edition were selected for their individual appeal and the variety they offer to the collection. The Opus 45 set is called *Melodious Etudes*, and Opus 46 *Progressive Etudes*; in general, the pieces within each set start with the easier ones and then gradually present more challenges. They range from intermediate level to rather advanced. The present volume starts with one of the best known of all, "The Avalanche"—a fairly easy piece that a child can play with brilliance, since one never has to cross the thumb. By the end of the volume ("Novelette"), the rich melodies and expansive figurations are more reminiscent of the mature scope of a Chopin ballade.

Here is a suggested sequence for studying the etudes, in four groupings:

Intermediate	op. 45/2, op. 45/9, op. 45/16, op. 46/7
Late Intermediate	op. 45/14, op. 45/15, op. 46/2
Early Advanced	op. 45/18, op. 45/19, op. 46/20, op. 46/5, op. 46/25
Advanced	op. 46/1, op. 46/12, op. 46/14, op. 46/29

Fingerings and pedaling indications throughout the volume are merely the editor's suggestions. The fingerings are designed to encourage healthy technique, especially as regards (1) strong and comfortable hand positions, and (2) active use of arm gestures in phrasing.

The spontaneity and individualism of Romanticism pervades Heller's studies, as it did all European music of the time. In that spirit, the editor's performance on the accompanying audio may not match every printed detail in the score. Anyone playing these pieces is encouraged to approach them rather freely as well, to indulge that inner spark of imagination. Our hope is that these polished creations will provide great satisfaction to players of any age, both for technical growth and as choice recital fare to share with audiences.

Notes on the Individual Studies

Melodious Etudes, Opus 45

Op. 45, No. 2 (The Avalanche)
Like many of the etudes, this rollicking piece encourages free, unrestrained arm movement—a key component of mature technique—as the triplet figure is rapidly tossed from left hand to right and back again. Craftily, Heller has constructed rapid passages that call only for strong fingers, with no thumb crossings at all. One of the most well-known of all his compositions, this etude produces a brilliant effect almost effortlessly.

Op. 45, No. 9 (Celestial Voices)
It is all too possible for students to emerge from a few years of piano lessons with the clichéd notion that melodies are always at the top of the overall texture, and lower notes should always play more quietly. Thankfully, Heller explores other possibilities, often writing etudes with melodies placed in the piano's rich middle range instead. In this piece, the right thumb is in the perfect register to boom out a full, dignified tune while the "heavenly" filigree floats above. Make this tonal contrast between melody and accompaniment quite obvious, even extreme; the effect remains beautiful, as long as one's wrist stays supple as it lends roundness to the deep singing tone. Due to its harmonic warmth and stately rhythm, this piece also provides an excellent exercise in *legato* pedaling.

Op. 45, No. 14 (Sailor's Song)
Players who have not yet developed a lot of facility can still create resonant sonorities with "Sailor's Song." The piece has strength and dignity. Its form is rather peculiar, since the two sections present essentially the same music with only slight variations in chord spellings and melodic details. It is almost as if Heller were proposing two versions of the same short piece. But the satisfying ending does sound much more final than anything that had come before.

Op. 45, No. 15 (Warrior's Song)
A crucial element of satisfying pianism is power—natural power from the shoulders, which can create grandeur without harshness of sound. The wide arcs created by both arms as they leap back and forth can encourage relaxation, along with an expansive sense that the entire keyboard is one's natural terrain. The 16th-note chords should be played healthily, with full sound.

Op. 45, No. 16 (Il Penseroso)
The Schubertian left-hand melody, in the piano's *cantabile* "cello" range, will linger in the mind for days. Enhanced right-hand figuration at the recapitulation (m. 26) typifies Heller's refined compositional touch.

Op. 45, No. 18 (Impatience)

Occasionally we find a perfect technical break-through piece for the budding pianist, and this is one such gem. Here is a chance to try for real brilliance in passagework—perhaps for the first time—and Heller brings it within reach by giving the right hand comfortable, sweeping scale runs that are well built for *crescendos* and speed. The stormy mood adds exciting drama.

Op. 45, No. 19 (Spinning Song)

Whether or not he had an actual spinning wheel in mind, Heller has crafted a classic finger-independence challenge (holding down certain fingers while articulating others) that happens to be a graceful musical vignette at the same time. With typical subtlety, he varies the left-hand sequence during the repeat of the A section.

Op. 45, No. 20 (The Ballet)

A refreshingly different texture characterizes this buoyant piece. From the beginning, the arm-staccatos in the left hand create bubbly energy, and the right hand's witty statements ride on that energy. The section starting at measure 68 offers an excellent chance to practice rotation technique in the left hand.

Progressive Etudes, Opus 46

Op. 46, No. 1 (Carefree)

This composition resembles the familiar, hard-working 16th-note etudes by Clementi and Cramer, which makes the proposed title "Carefree" an interesting choice. The oscillating parts of the passagework necessitate wrist rotation at quite specific moments—a useful technique to master. If the *staccatos* in the other hand are played in a crisp, lively way, there is considerable charm in the texture. Heller skillfully gives right and left hands equal tasks to carry out, yielding equal technical benefits.

Op. 46, No. 2 (The Anvil)

This title can be quite helpful, since it encourages a solid, well-grounded tempo in which fingers can negotiate the passagework healthily, with firmness and sparkle.

Op. 46, No. 5 (The Wind)

Similarly, this title seems to inspire a deeper technical approach. Instead of flighty, perhaps insubstantial thirty-second note passages, the vivid ⊂ ⊃ idea evoked by the image of "wind" helps each hand fill out the running notes with a generous shape. This can enhance technical security. Rotation can be used liberally here as well, with good technical benefit.

Op. 46, No. 7 (Petite Tarantelle)

Short, to the point, and highly entertaining. Not a note is wasted in this showy and rather easy-to-play character piece. The form is a bit unusual: an introduction takes us to m. 17, where the customary A-B-A form actually starts. Students might find their fingers inadvertently racing due to the music's whirling energy, but a *giusto* tempo, together with crisp *staccato* chords, will yield a steadier and more attractive result.

Op. 46, No. 12 (Shimmering Waters)

Heller's elegance of design is evidenced here by the subtle, creative ways in which musical material is altered. In the final recapitulation, the new A-sharp in m. 38 adds harmonic spice, the added right-hand pickup notes in the last beat of m. 39 propels the momentum forward, and the bass octaves from m. 40 to the end create a triumphant conclusion. Chopin was known to use quite similar touches to vary music when it was repeated. This etude calls for mastery of liquid, shapely passagework.

Op. 46, No. 14 (Song of the Sea)

Varying left-hand figures (compare m. 1 with m. 13) make this stirring composition slightly more challenging than it might otherwise have been. Perhaps the most unexpected compositional touch is the expansive coda (m. 60 to the end).

The long string of *staccatos* in the coda may be more readily learned if they are mentally bracketed into logical groupings, for example:

Study, Op. 46 No. 14, m. 60

Op. 46, No. 25 (Song of the Gondolier)
Another warm-hearted melody delivered by thumbs in the middle range, while figurations wreathe above. Since both hands share the tune this time, it takes careful practice to match their sounds and eliminate undesired melodic "bumps." The right-hand fingering at m. 17 might surprise some players, but crossing the thumb to a black key can work with remarkable naturalness. The writing in this lyrical piece asks both arms to inscribe balletic arcs in the air, which is a liberating experience once it becomes familiar. Memorization is essential; it is almost impossible to play this piece with any fluency until this is done and one's eyes can train themselves on the keyboard and the pervasive acrobatics of the arms.

Op. 46, No. 29 (Novelette)
The sweeping gestures here invite an expansive, mature way of addressing the keyboard. Since the right-hand figures usually start with a sixteenth rest, it falls to the left hand to establish convincing rhythmic control throughout. The unusual tonality of D-flat major places many of the passages squarely on the black keys; when a player has found comfort and virtuosity there, this study has served its purpose well. The ending is notably extroverted and brilliant, and the editor suggests substituting the following chord for the left hand in m. 58.

Study, Op. 46 No. 29, m. 58, l.h.

—*William Westney*

SELECTED STUDIES
Opus 45

Study in A Minor
The Avalanche

Stephen Heller
Op. 45, No. 2

Study in E Major
Celestial Voices

Stephen Heller
Op. 45, No. 9

Study in F Major

Sailor's Song

Stephen Heller
Op. 45, No. 14

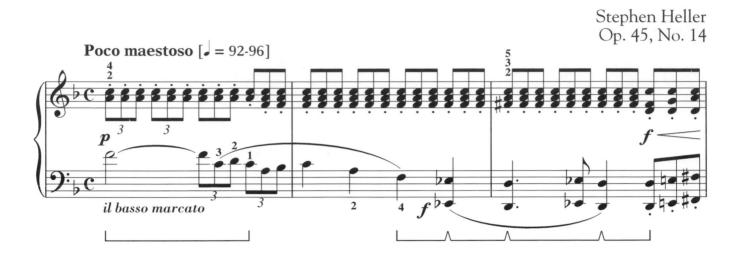

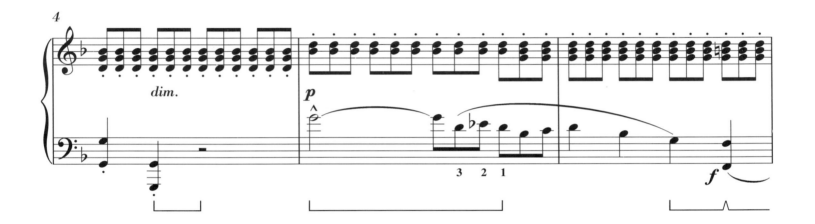

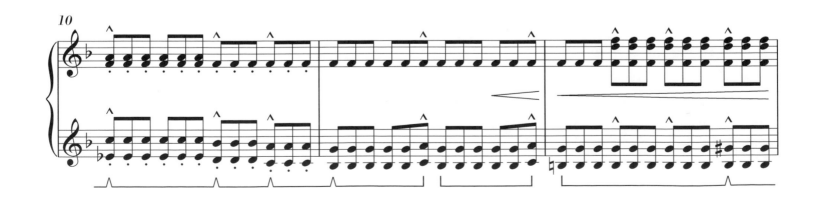

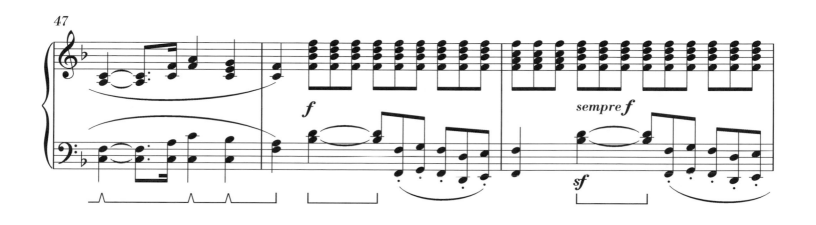

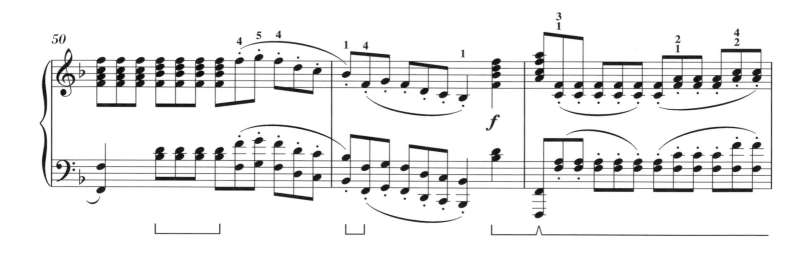

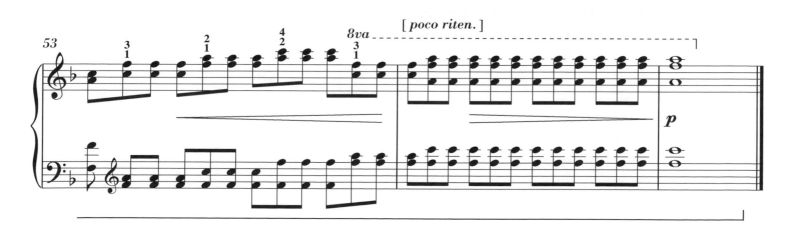

Study in D Minor
Warrior's Song

Stephen Heller
Op. 45, No. 15

Study in B-flat Major

Il Penseroso

Stephen Heller
Op. 45, No. 16

Andantino con tenerezza [♩ = 86-96]

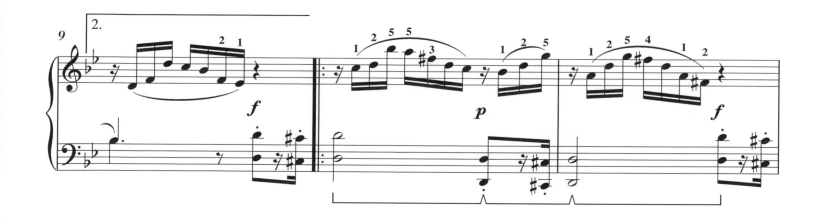

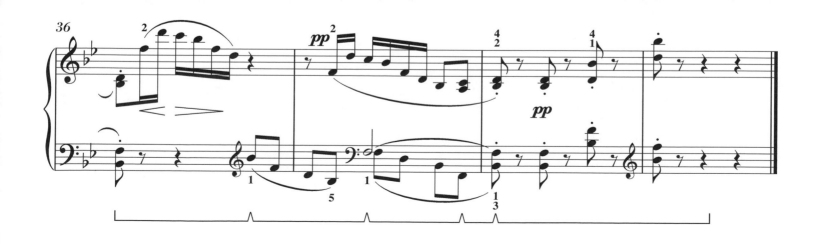

Study in G Minor

Impatience

Stephen Heller
Op. 45, No. 18

[*With brief touches of pedal*]

Study in F Major
Spinning Song

Stephen Heller
Op. 45, No. 19

Study in E Major
The Ballet

Stephen Heller
Op. 45, No. 20

SELECTED STUDIES
Opus 46

Study in C Major
Carefree

Stephen Heller
Op. 46, No. 1

Allegro assai ($\quad$ = 132-152)

Study in G Major
The Anvil

Stephen Heller
Op. 46, No. 2

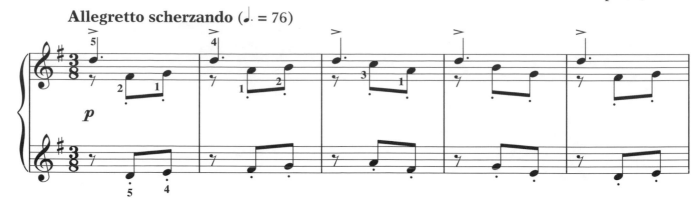

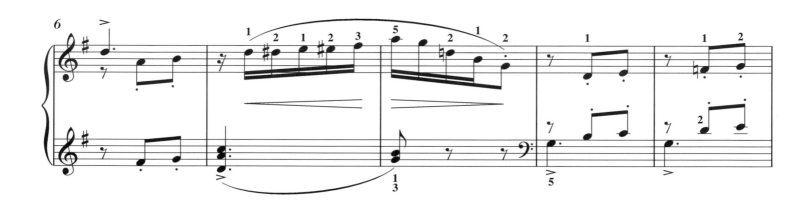

Study in C Minor
The Wind

Stephen Heller
Op. 46, No. 5

Study in E Minor
Petite Tarantelle

Stephen Heller
Op. 46, No. 7

Study in D Major
Shimmering Waters

Stephen Heller
Op. 46, No. 12

Study in D Minor
Song of the Sea

Stephen Heller
Op. 46, No. 14

Study in F Major
Song of the Gondolier

Stephen Heller
Op. 46, No. 25

Allegretto con moto [♩ = 72-76]

Study in D-flat Major
Novelette

Stephen Heller
Op. 46, No. 29

* See Performance Notes, p. 8

ABOUT THE EDITOR

WILLIAM WESTNEY

Pianist **William Westney** came to prominence as the top piano prize-winner of the Geneva International Competition, and he appeared thereafter in European television broadcasts and as soloist with such major orchestras as l'Orchestre de la Suisse Romande and the Houston, San Antonio, and New Haven Symphonies. His solo recital appearances include New York's Lincoln Center, the National Gallery, and Phillips Collection in Washington, D.C., St. John's Smith Square in London, National Public Radio ("Performance Today"), Taiwan, Korea, and a U.S. State Department tour of Italy. Critics have praised his recordings of solo and chamber works for CRI and Musical Heritage Society, and *Newsweek* magazine selected his CRI recording of Leo Ornstein's works as one of its "Ten Best American Music Recordings" of the year.

Dr. Westney holds a Bachelor of Arts degree from Queens College in New York and a Masters and Doctorate in performance from Yale University, all with highest academic and pianistic honors. He was awarded a Fulbright grant for study in Italy, and while there, was the only American winner in auditions held by *Radiotelevisione Italiana*. His piano teachers have included Leopold Mittman, Donald Currier, Paul Baumgartner, and Claude Frank.

An internationally noted educator, William Westney has held two endowed positions at Texas Tech University—Paul Whitfield Horn Distinguished Professor and Browning Artist-in-Residence—and has been honored many times with teaching awards, including the Yale School of Music Alumni Association's prestigious "Certificate of Merit" for his distinctive and innovative contributions to the teaching of musical performance. He has also been a frequent guest professor at Tonghai University in Taiwan.

Dr. Westney's unique "Un-Master Class" performance workshops were described as "fascinating" in a featured *New York Times* article. They are in demand throughout the U.S. and abroad, and are frequently held at such prominent centers as the Aspen School, Peabody Conservatory, Kennedy Center, Royal Conservatory (Toronto), Cleveland Institute, Tanglewood Institute, Royal College of Music (London), *Universität für Musik und darstellende Kunst* (Vienna), and the Juilliard School.

Amadeus Press released William Westney's first book, *The Perfect Wrong Note*, in Fall 2003 to critical acclaim. According to the *Library Journal*, it is a "well-thought-out approach to music instruction to which many aspire, but which few attain," and *American Record Guide* described it as "refreshing and rewarding."